BIOLOGICAL BATTERY

The Q-Experience

by
Dr. Howard Peiper

Recharge Your Biological Battery Revised Edition

Dr. Howard Peiper

Copyright ©2002

Cover design by Shawn Williams, graphics@q2.com.au

No part of this book may be reproduced in any form without the written consent of the publisher.

ISBN 0-9702964-2-8
Library of Congress Catalog Card Number 2002116783
Revised edition November 2003

Printed in USA

Recharge Your Biological Battery is not intended as medical advice. It is written solely for informational and educational purposes. Please consult a health professional should the need for one be indicated. Because there is always some risk involved, the author and publisher are not responsible for any adverse effects or consequences resulting from the use of any of the suggestions, preparations, or methods described in this book. The publisher does not advocate the use of any particular diet or health program, but believes the information presented in this book should be available to the public.

ATN Publishing
561 Shunpike Rd.
Sheffield, MA 01257
413-229-7935

Foreword

*If we are beings of energy,
then it follows that we can be affected by energy.*

Quantum Field Science asks that we see all life, organic and inorganic, as a vast network of energetic fields that work together in a wonderfully paradoxical way. The paradox is that while this network is incredibly complex and intricate, it is also easily accessible and changeable. When we apply this philosophy to our bodies and to our lives, we begin to see the enormity of the self-empowerment that this understanding of life gives us.

We are essentially a complex network of energy waves, which create and change moment by moment, our bodies, lives, and our world. Every part of our body is made up of this energy "substance," and in fact, every organ, tissue and cell vibrates or resonates at specific frequencies.

Quantum Field Science sees human beings as networks of complex energy fields that interface with physical and cellular systems. By rebalancing the energy fields, Quantum Field Science allows the individuals own innate intelligence to restore order.

This remarkable book by Dr. Howard Peiper shows that there is a connection between conventional medicine and Quantum Field Science. Dr. Peiper explains that if our interlocking energy systems become imbalanced, there may be pathological symptoms that show up on a physcial, emotional, mental and spiritual level.

Recharge your Biological Battery helps us understand that when the energy levels are lowered, the body becomes weakened. These imbalances can be corrected utilizing the Q2 Experience technology. Dr. Peiper's book brilliantly explains that the Quantum Field Science will not only give future doctors a different view on the causes of dis-ease, but also show more effective ways by which we can remain well.

I.G.Olarsch, N.D.

Kirlian Photographs of cells

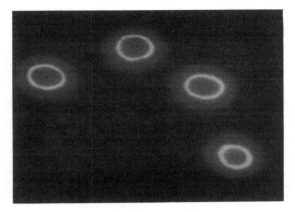

Before the Q2 experience

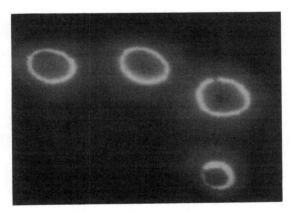

After the Q2 experience

Kirlian Photos
Courtesy of Gerry and Janice Parsons
Rutherfordton, NC

Research conducted by Lana J. Ford, Ph.D., Institute of Integrative Health
143 Woodview Dr., Rutherfordton, NC 28139 (828) 287-0955

Table of Contents

Foreword	3
1. Healing Waters	9
2. What is Vibrational Medicine?	11
3. Quantum Field Science	15
4. Detoxification of the Body	19
5. The Spark of Life	23
6. The Q2 Water Energy System	27
7. Electrolytes	33
8. What People are Saying About the Q2	35
A. Research Report	50
Resource Directory	51

Healing Waters

Sacred, or healing, waters have always existed and have been mentioned and used by many diverse religious and spiritual traditions. Can these healing waters perform miracles? Yes, but not in the way many people traditionally thought—that God was intervening to accomplish a supernatural feat. Water, as we know, is an excellent conductor of electricity. Many researchers have recently referred to water as having an *energy and vibrational memory*. Water can imprint, store, and transmit specific energy/vibrational holograms, which it receives from music, from human thoughts and emotions, and from the universe's specific places that are high in cosmo-teluric energies.

Since our body is 70-80 percent water, when such *vibrational waters* touch or enter our bodies they transmit by resonance their "energy/vibrational hologram" to the water already present in our bodies, raising its vibrational and energy structure. This naturally sets in motion the healing or reharmonization process. Some *vibrational waters* are already well known; those where Marian apparitions have occurred, such as at Lourdes, Ste. Anne de Beaupres, or Medjugorje. Sacred writings teach us that there are other bodies of water that have been imprinted by the rays of the moon, the planets, or the constellations at special times. They explain that these waters have been exposed to rituals, blessings, or strong thoughts and energy that normal water lacks. This signature cannot be picked up at the chemical level (it is still H_2O like all water), but it can be measured in terms of its energy-vibrational frequencies. These are the subtle agents carried by water that actively affect changes in our bodies and psyches. Water, in fact, can pick up our energy, such as when we take a bath.

Each person has existing within their cellular structure, a blueprint for health. In the course of our lives, this blueprint may be altered resulting in illness. *Vibrational water* interacts with existing water present in our body and may restore the original imprinted vibration of health. When the sick cell listens to the "suggestion" of the new imprint from the vibrational water, it begins to respond transforming itself so as to reacquire its original health frequency.

While living in Florida, I would frequently visit the Warm Mineral Springs. These springs are another example of *healing waters*. People from around the world would bathe in the springs and notice changes either on a physical or a mental plane. *Healing water* sites are useful to facilitate cleansing the body of toxins (chemical drugs, commercial food, heavy metals, etc.) or electromagnetic fields from quartz watches, cell phones, computers, etc. *Healing waters* are also sometimes called memory waters in that they are able to restore cellular equilibrium and reset the balance of our energy body on its electromagnetic axis.

In all cases, *vibrational healing water* communicates its own holographic, energy/vibrational imprint to the water present in the body of the person. This basically raises the vibrational energy and consciousness level of the person. Specifically, it harmonizes and enhances the proper functioning of the immune, hormonal, nervous, and circulatory systems, which then restore proper equilibrium and a higher level of mental, physical, and spiritual health. The Q2 Water Energy System has found a way to replicate these healing waters and may well prove to be one of the great health technological developments of the 21st century.

2
What is Vibrational Medicine?

The use of vibrational medicine is certainly not new. Many disciplines of healing such as Chinese Medicine, Ayurvedic (Eastern) Indian Medicine, Homeopathy, and Charismatic Healing (such as laying on of hands and/or healing by prayer) have understood the energetic nature of body/mind/spirit for centuries. Vibrational (also called Energetic) Medicine invites us to look at our world and ourselves in a completely new way. The science from which modern or conventional medical models are derived is based on Newtonian Physics. This model believes that human and animal species are nothing more than elaborate machines. When viewed mechanistically, our bodies are seen as material forms, and energy is given very little attention.

With the advent of twentieth-century physics, a new understanding and paradigm emerged and the seeds of Quantum Physics were born. Einstein turned the scientific world on its ear with his Theory of Relativity, which essentially stated that light, energy, and matter are all of equal importance. Where matter in the Newtonian model once ruled, energy and quantum physics are now taking its place. However, this understanding of the universe is slow to find its way into the science of medicine because the means to prove these theories in terms of human beings and health is difficult.

Within the past thirty years, technological advances have opened the door for the study of energy and how it behaves. The results of these studies are creating a paradigm shift.
- In the Quantum universe, everything is energy!
- Energy precedes matter and matter accounts for only 2 percent of the Universe!
- The word *energy* often makes people uncomfortable because we can't see it, yet we all know that energy exists. We know that sound comes through our radios via radio or sound waves. We know that we can see pictures of the body using

radioactive energy or Xrays. And we know the solar energy from the sun; we feel its warmth and can even see its rays streaming forth to light our days.
- Quantum Physics asks that we see all life and matter as a vast network of energetic fields that work together in a wonderful paradoxical way. When we see its relevance to our lives, we begin to see how important the ramifications are.

If we can take these familiar ideas regarding energy and expand them a bit, we can come to understand more about the energetic nature of our world and ourselves. As we begin to understand how Vibrational Medicine can help us, let us define disease as an altered or distorted resonance level within the body or organ system (*Dis-ease*) Healing takes place when that resonance level is restored to its original, non-distorted or altered level.

Our perception of disease must be changed from our viewpoint that by naming diseases, we think of them as conditions that we have, to viewing *Dis-ease* as a process, or something that we are going through. Instead of saying "I have cancer," we need to say something like, "I am cancering," or "I am tumoring." Psychologically, this implies that we are in a state that we are moving through, not one in which we are irretrievably stuck.

The other thing to consider is that we have been taught to view our pains and disease symptoms as bad things, when in fact we need be looking at the fact that our body is communicating to us—trying to get our attention to fix a problem. We have forgotten how truly brilliant our physical bodies are at keeping us going. The pains and symptoms we experience are simply signals from the body, telling us that we need to pay attention to an abnormal condition. To keep us functioning properly, our body will compensate as long as it can until it runs out of "steam." At that point we receive a signal usually in the form of pain or discomfort. If we ignore these warning signals, we may escalate the condition until we are in crisis. Then we finally decide to take action, which usually translates into calling the doctor and assigning them the task of healing us. When we give up responsibility for our own health and wellbeing, we have given away our power to heal ourselves.

Taking back responsibility for our health can be illustrated by the following testimonial:

"Because of prior auto accidents, I have incurred many injuries that conventional medicine cannot seem to help. For example, I still suffer from osteoarthritis, herniated discs, stinosis, bones that have not healed properly and a spinal cord injury. I also have Type II Diabetes, high blood pressure, kidney stones, and for an unknown reason, blood in my urine. Last August, I learned of the Q2 from a friend of mine. On the first treatment, I felt pulsing in all the areas where I suffered trauma as well as through my feet and fallen arches. The energy moved up my legs and into my whole body. I bought my own Q2 and followed the protocol (every other day) for several months.

The results were amazing. There is no more blood in my urine and after only two treatments my kidney stones are gone. I can rotate my left wrist completely, which I previously was unable to do. I have more strength in both hands, the edema is totally gone, and I can go freely up and down stairs without any pain. My mental abilities have increased and I am able to focus, use the computer and be responsible. What my allopathic doctor was supposed to do for me, the Q2 has done."
-Marj Fish, Temecula, Ca.

Vibrational Medicine uses various tools and therapies to create, manage, and enhance our body's resonance levels. Since everything is composed of energy—and energy precedes matter—we can deduce that *everything* falls into the category of Vibrational Medicine. This includes conventional medical techniques.

Note: The difference between one tool and another is the degree to which they create unwanted or detrimental side effects.

Allopathic models are not about *healthcare*, but rather are about *Dis-ease care* or symptom relief. As you treat one problem you may actually be initiating other problems because you are disturbing the vibrational balance of the other energy systems within the body. A good way to visualize this is to imagine that the body has rivers of energy running through it—meridians, or the established acupuncture pathways of Chinese Medicine. If you have for example, a gallbladder attack and the surgeon removes your gallbladder, he or she has essentially disrupted or dammed the energy flow for that particular energy pathway. When there is no more gallbladder, bodily functions downstream are now cut off from the *energy river*. This causes the body upstream from the block to become backed up with excess energy.

3
Quantum Field Science

Quantum Field Science is a common phrase to people all around the world, yet this may be the first time you have heard of it. Quantum Field Science is adding a whole new dimension to alternative health. Its plausibility is transforming skeptics into believers at an amazing rate. So what exactly is Quantum Field Science? What does it do? And why is it so important to so many people all around the world? The purpose of this book is not only to answer such questions but also to inform people of Quantum Field Science and how it applies itself to matters of health.

Since the dawn of mankind there has been sickness—plagues, small pox, cholera, yellow fever, and tuberculosis. The advent of antibiotics resulted in these types of health problems being rendered virtually nonexistent. However, it seems that even without such plagues we are still suffering from an unbelievable number of illnesses that have no available cures. What is even more interesting is that many of the fatal illnesses of today are not even contagious. Terminal and serious diseases seem to be striking a much larger number of people than ever before. The need for effective healers and new cures is as important as it has ever been.

Cancer is striking more and more people each year, as is heart disease, diabetes, AIDS, and many other life-threatening illnesses. New breeds of diseases are being discovered as well, and it seems that we catch colds and the flu more frequently. Even our essential body organs are no longer functioning properly as statistics of people with kidney failure, lung disease, liver disease, and much more confirm.

What is the reason for this slow degradation of our health? And what can we do to repair the damage that has already been done? There are many contributing factors to health problems. Unfortunately, it seems that many people simply have little or no concern at all for the state of their health. We know the world has changed dramatically in the last thousand years. No longer do we rely on our feet or on horses for our main means of transportation, nor do we have to wait six months to reach a destination far across the sea. Humankind has made such advancement in the realm of science and technology that society seems miraculous. With all the many conveniences that we have gained in this modern society, it seems we have also lost a great deal as well.

Now, instead of the peaceful sounds of nature that once could be heard so clearly, we are plagued by a constant low buzzing of electricity in the air. Instead of taking a breath of clean fresh air, our lungs are filled with the smog from cities. The quality, too, of our fresh fruit and vegetables has changed. Who doesn't notice the change in their taste? Science has played a role in the indiscriminate use of food additives and chemical sprays for crops. City water is treated chemically and noise pollution, the irradiation of food, and nuclear weapons testing adds to the list of hazards. Electro-smog from microwave signals, radio frequencies, cell towers, and affect us without being seen. It has already been established that toxins come in many different forms and disguises but every single one has an adverse effect on the human body.

Toxins affect the human body in far more serious ways producing symptoms much more serious than just a bad case of acne. When toxins are ingested they are detected by the body's state of health. Once the body has detected this dangerous substance, its primary objective is to purge these toxins as quickly as possible and so the cellular cleansing begins totally without input from our conscious mind. The human body is a marvelous creature and has its own natural ways of breaking down and purging toxins and waste. For example, the liver, the kidneys, the spleen, the pancreas, and the lymphatic system each play a very important part in this process.

The body pushes toxins out through the skin in the form of perspiration and skin blemishes, or removes them through our normal digestive waste disposal systems. However, when there is a constant bombardment of toxins being poured into our systems, these organs need to work overtime. The excess energy expended in this process causes our organs to tire. Sometimes this extra work causes damage prohibiting the organ from functioning properly. This halts the purging process and toxins continue to build up causing illness and inhibiting the body's natural function. As this ingesting and purging of toxins is a never-ending cycle, there is a constant drain on the body's energy supply. The constant depletion of energy and the overuse of the body's defense systems, leaves less energy resources to fight off more serious illnesses, or even to heal wounds.

So, what can be done about the already large build up of toxins in our body? How do we restore our body's functions to their full capability again? Perhaps dealing with this build up of toxins may be easier than you think. Throughout the ages, there is at least one thing that has never changed, and that is mankind's search for ways to heal the injured and cure the ill. In the very early days, tribes, towns, and villages did not have doctors equipped with the technology of today. These early peoples did have healers—in the form of Shamans, Medicine Men, Apothecaries, Herbalists, and even White Witches. These healers were all knowledgeable in the healing properties of plants and herbs, minerals, and even some precious metals and stones. Their herbal potions and poultices had tremendous healing qualities and the infant stages of modern medicine were based on these natural-healing remedies. One of the many ancient natural therapies was a very early form of *bio-magnetic healing*. This involved the use of the lodestone. The lodestone was ground to a powder and mixed with water and certain other precious metals. When this mixture was applied to the affected area, not necessarily to the point of pain, it was found to be magical in its curative abilities.

Today, we have Quantum Field Science, which is a terminology given to a new type of physical science that completely replaces the current atomic model, allowing the possibility of explaining all actions and functions including anomalies and chaotic functionality. Current theories give the user the ability to mathematically explain the functionality of certain aspects of the known universe, but fail to anticipate and/or explain seemingly random chaotic functions that occur. The reason being that the base construct that is currently seen as the foundation of existence is in fact incorrect—that function, energy, and matter are seen as separate entities that coexist rather than being seen as the same material viewed from differing perspectives.

Example of Quantum Field Science in action:

Pictures of an autistic child's progress when treated with the Q2 Water Energy System.

Before treatment (January 2000)   After treatment (April 2000)

Please refer to page 37 for the complete description by Pedro V. DeCosta of the progress of a seven-year old boy who used the Q2 bath every other day prior to his occupational therapy sessions.

4
Detoxification of the Body

In order for us to know the body detoxifies itself, we need to understand a little about how the body functions and in particular how our cells work. While there are many cells in our body that perform different functions and have different internal structures they all have some basic function similarities. All our cells need water to survive and work and they all have three basic components (excluding red blood cells that eject their nucleus). These components are the nucleus, the internal structure, and the plasma membrane. Each of these components, when combined, performs specific functions and although each of their functions are individual they all intake water, metabolize it, and eject a waste product called nucleic acid. This waste product is then dealt with through the body's main cleaning systems—the liver and the kidneys. If this flow-through system is not adhered to problems can occur, such as the cell becoming clogged with toxins. A correctly functioning cell has a good flow of liquid (water) going through it, entering and leaving the cell structure through the outer cell membrane.

The outer cell membrane, or plasma membrane, is a selectively permeable barrier, meaning that it allows some substances to pass while excluding others. When a substance can penetrate the plasma membrane without any energy input from the cell, it is called passive transport. When the cell must provide metabolic energy the process is called active transport. The movement of water into the cell is an example of passive transport, while movement of amino acids and ions across the membrane is active transport. The plasma membrane as well as being selectively permeable has another very important function. It maintains a potential voltage difference between the internal structure of the cell and the intercellular fluid.

Scientists are just now starting to realize the importance of the voltage that exists on the membrane itself. Its electrical value plays a part in helping the membrane be selectively permeable. If this voltage drops too low, it contributes to loss of cell integrity. What is important here is that it has been scientifically proven that an unhealthy cell has a very poor membrane voltage.

There are a lot of things that can start to go wrong when we exert an outside influence on the cell, such as a toxin attack. Our bodies are more than capable of withstanding low levels of toxins, but when these levels rise too high a chain of events starts to take place and the integrity of the cell is compromised. The cell structure can be affected from both the outside and the inside. Toxins that cause problems do not need to come from an external source because the cell itself produces a waste product that could be considered a toxin.

The body has a natural defense mechanism for removing toxins from the system. In the average individual these systems are functioning correctly, but under load (stress or illness), the system can break down and result in a toxin build up. For most people the threat of toxin build up is from the type of external hazards we are now exposed to, not from having our internal cleaning system operating incorrectly. Some toxins do not remain in the intercellular fluid, and therefore they become attached to the cell membrane. If the body is operating below 100 percent this can cause problems in many ways. There are however a few basic causes that help us understand how the body becomes toxic and how we can resolve the problem. We can help the body cope using its own natural processes. Three examples of how the body becomes toxic in relation to the effect it has on the cell are:

1. Toxification by natural waste products that is built up of nucleic waste from the cell.
2. Toxification by low-level artificial toxins—man-made compounds.
3. Toxification causing genetic alteration—genetically engineered materials.

It needs to be noted that although these processes are listed individually they can and do all occur simultaneously.

To detach toxins that have affixed themselves to the cell we can employ the usage of a unique device. Based upon an interpretation of Quantum Theory, the Q2 Water Energy System unit was developed to provide an external source of compatible energy for the body. Developed by Terry Skrinjar in Australia, the unit is not a medical device and does not actually diagnose, cure, or treat any disease or condition. It energizes the water, which is used as a conductive medium. All living things possess energy fields, thus when a person bathes in the water and takes a Q2 Water Energy System bath, the body absorbs the energy provided to use as needed. Since the quality of design and manufacture are of medical grade and the unit is used in water, the Q2 Water Energy System has received official approval from the TGA in Australia, (Australian equivalent to the FDA) and is marketed there as a therapeutic device.

The Q2 Water Energy System enhances the bio-energy of your cells. As discussed earlier, the cells in your body contain an electric charge. This charge is not like the electricity you are familiar with like which is used in your home. The first thing the unit does is to increase the charge on the plasma membrane surrounding the cell. This applies to all cells throughout the body. It also has an effect on the internal structure of the cell as well because the electrical energy being supplied to the cell is compatible with the metabolic energy of the cell. This effectively increases the available metabolic energy the cell can function with. Once this is achieved a number of things start to happen.

By increasing the electrical value of the cell membrane, we also increase the value of the electrical field that results from the electrical potential on the cell membrane itself. Boosting and extending this field to the proper parameters affects the toxins that have attached themselves to the cell membrane. It also helps restore integrity to the actual membrane itself, by allowing restoration of the plasma membrane's function of selective permeability. Restoring proper cell function increases the body's ability to process the toxins properly again. The liver and kidneys can now begin to remove more of the toxins reducing the load on the rest of the systems.

Once the toxins are detached from the cell membrane they are free to be moved by the intercellular fluid. The body's natural processes, with these extra resources, can take over and remove the toxin through normal systems. This also has the effect of once again letting clean intercellular fluid flow correctly through the membrane. With an increase in the metabolic energy now available to the cell, the cell and the intercellular fluid are now restored to normal function. With the cell in a much healthier state, and now having an increased metabolic level of energy, it can begin to function properly. Toxins that have entered the cell during its poor health state can now be purged and actively transported from the internal structure. The extra energy input to the cell now available makes this process possible again.

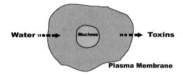

Healthy Cell

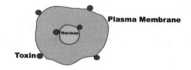

Unhealthy Cell

The Spark of Life

The body is a bioelectric organism. Its trillions of cells produce and use electricity as their driving force, or *life force*. Bioelectricity is generated by the cellular exchange of negatively and positively charged particles called ions. These ions are formed when minerals, which have been broken down by the stomach's hydrochloric acid, come together in body fluids. A tiny electrical charge is generated when potassium is released from inside a cell and is replaced with sodium. When the current has passed, the potassium is pumped back into the cell and sodium is pumped out.

Dr. Lendon Smith explains,[1] "In this way the cells act as tiny batteries with their own electromagnetic current. The collection of all these electrical forces about the trillions of our cells constitutes our energy system. It is this subtle energy that produces life. Fatigue may be that the batteries have run down." The body's dependence on electrical charges has never been in dispute, but scientists are now beginning to understand the vital role it plays in the various systems in the body. A medical team at Geneva's University Hospital has discovered that white blood cells can produce electricity,[2] which will help research understand better how the human body fights microbes.

Until Dr. Jacques Schrenzel, Dr. Karl-Heinz Krause, and their colleagues at the Geneva Hospital's Infectious Diseases Division unraveled the mystery, it was not known how the cells generate the body's lethal weapon against invading bacteria and fungi—toxic oxygen radical superoxide. The Geneva team reported it had identified an enzyme in nature (NADPH oxidase) that generates electron currents through cellular membranes. These currents, which are identical to those that light an electric bulb but

---

[1] Smith, Lendon, *Feed Your Kids Right*, Keats Publishing, 1986.
[2] Natures Journal #392, pp. 734-737, 1998.

ten billion times smaller, convert oxygen to the microbe-killing superoxide.

The discovery made by the Geneva medical team helps to explain why the Q2 Water Energy System aids healing and has the potential to eliminate bacteria and fungi infections. Because the potential voltage in the cell membrane is increased, the potential of the immune system can be substantially enhanced. This effect also aids in prevention by maintaining the effectiveness of the cellular function.

Live Blood Tests

There is no doubt that energy changes are made in the body. One of the most noticeable is the effect the Q2 has on blood. The photographs below illustrate dramatic changes are made without even altering diet or lifestyle.

Fig. 1

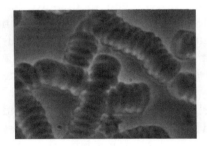 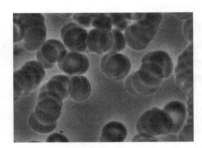

Before   After

The samples in Figure 2 were taken from a male smoker. After two weeks using the Q2 Water Energy System, improvement is quite obvious. Very measurable real differences also occur with blood pressure as elevated blood pressures tend to fall while low blood pressures increase. The evidence that healthy blood can improve health is not debated.

Fig 2.

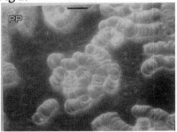 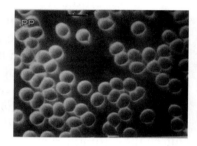

Before   After

The samples in Figure 3 were taken from a 35-year male. On the left, blood cells are flat and chained. On the right the cells are now round and a lot healthier. The Q2 Water Energy System achieved this with only three sessions.

Fig. 3

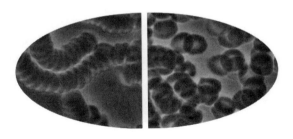

Before   After

Daniel Reid, author of *The Tao of Detox*,[3] explains that when the body's bio-energy field has been recharged and rebalanced by the externally generated bio electric field of the Q2 Water Energy Spa, the physical body responds immediately to the properly balanced signals by detoxifying, and repairing itself. The Q2 therapy may be applied in a foot, hand or full bath, with equally effective results.

In an article from a 2001 issue of Explore Magazine[4], Dr. Timothy Ray says, "According to Dr. H. Schimmel, world famous energetic physician from Germany, when the nanoamperage of the body measured at all of the end points of the acupuncture meridians is below 400 nA (normal is 400-800nA) there is a focal disturbance. In most of these focal patients the Darkfield microscopy reveals that the zeta potential of the RBC membrane has lost its negative charge as evidenced by the appearance of rouleaux and/or aggregation (diminished oxygen, nutrient and waste exchange). I have repeatedly treated people with low battery conditions with the Q2 Energy Spa using reverse osmosis water remineralized with pure potassium citrate, and have seen their nanoamperage come up into normal range within and under the recommended treatment time when measured immediately after the treatment."

---

[3] Reid, Daniel, *The Tao of Detox*, Chapter 9 High-Tech Electro-Detox, Cygnus Books 2003

[4] Ray, Timothy, OMD, L.Ac, *The Low Battery Focus*, Explore, Vol 10, #4, 2001.

6
The Q2 Water Energy System

The Q2 Water Energy System is a unit that when placed into water is capable of generating a bio-energy field similar to that of any water based vessel (that which contains water). Since the only naturally occurring substance with an energy field is water, the unit is used in water. Creating a field with these properties cannot be done simply. It requires a process that already has some of the unique frequencies present in it. The water interacts with an electric current to produce the biocharge. While the water is a very important part of the process, a magnetic field is needed to make it work properly. Passing electrical current between specially designed plates in the water creates the magnetic field. The resultant biocharge is the product of a combination of the water, electricity, metal, and magnetism. Advantages of creating such a field are that its usage on a living organism generates minimum disruption, and completely negates side effects that are all too common with things artificial (organic vs. inorganic).

The Q2 unit was designed and constructed to generate a magnetic field structure of multiple frequencies set up by an electric current passing through the unit, using water as the medium to create the electric circuit. With water as the medium, the structure is set for the magnetic field—meaning that it creates a field containing the base frequencies of the water. This also causes the water to be able to convert the artificial electrical energy into a bio-energy, which has the necessary frequencies that make the energy available to you. Since our body is mostly water, energy based on these frequencies is readily accepted.

Everybody has his or her own unique personal bio-signature, which means each person's frequency is a little different from the next persons. The Q2 instantly adjusts to the person's frequency. The amazing properties of water are how this is achieved. It works because water contains the natural base frequencies that are present in the body. Not all frequencies needed are there, but they are very close. Water is an active substance, so when water come in contract with something, the frequency of what it contacts is integrated into its own frequency structure. Because the body is mostly made of water, the ability to interact is very high. When the body is immersed in water, the frequency of the body is instantly added to the water because the biocharge when induced, copies the frequencies already in the water. This is why only one person can use the unit at a time. Each treatment helps to balance the body's energy meridians, and realign the energy field. Creating a *rebalancing* of these energy lines allows the body to function better.

Water is important because it is the most active ingredient in our body and affects our whole constitution. The water in our body is also very active with electrical charges. There is however a big difference between the electrical charges in our body and the electricity we use in our homes. If you try to use the electricity straight from the power outlet at home it will cause serious damage to the body because:
1. It is an AC current
2. It is the wrong frequency for the body
3. It has the wrong electrical format

Water contains electricity, but it is dissimilar to AC electricity. Good, clean healthy water contains a basic electrical biocharge. This biocharge can be identified because it has very distinct cycles, or charge fluctuations, that can be measured. When the charge cycles are measured, it takes 17 minutes and 1 second before it starts to repeat again. This is very important and one of the reasons why time limits are set for the Q2. The period that has been set is from 20 minutes to 35 minutes. If 20 minutes is set, only 1 cycle is used, but if 35 minutes is set then 2 cycles are used.

Another factor to consider is that water does not have either a sine wave (AC current's frequency is about 50hz. It is called a sine wave and is not suitable for direct application to the body), nor a square wave DC pulse (alters pulse frequency measurements). Water has a biocharge pattern where the voltages are constantly changing along with the period of frequency inside the one complete cycle. Therefore, a biocharge contains patterns within patterns. It is almost impossible to replicate this signal, digitally, and even harder to create the constantly changing patterns in any body. This is what sets the Q2 Water Energy System into a class of its own—it can!

The Q2 unit works as a charger for the body. However, the process it uses is not linear but algorithmic, which means that it charges the body in stages or steps. The body begins by being able to absorb a large charge when it is first used, and then as more charging is applied the absorption rate becomes less. The charging process can be equated to the lunar cycle, which is 29.5 days, and this is why it is recommended that the unit be used for at least 1 month (28 days) for the first time.

Since each person is unique, the charge cycle is going to be different. The starting point for the charge cycle depends on the age of a person and his/her health status. If the person has a low health status, the Q2 system may improve it. The strength and frequency of the human bioelectrical field is the major factor in the human body's immune system. Magnetic resonant frequencies of any invading organism be it viral, bacterial, or fungal, cannot take hold in a body that has a higher level. An organism will still try to invade and adapt to the body's higher energy field, which is why more virulent strains evolve over time. The body's secondary immune system—namely antibodies—comes into action when the invading organism's magnetic resonant frequency level is strong enough to survive in the body's magnetic energy field. For larger organisms or more direct contact such as wounds from cuts or splinters, the white blood cells become the first line of defense for the body.

The field generated by the Q2 unit overrides that of the invading organism, neutralizing it and allowing the bodies natural elimination organs (skin, liver, and kidneys) to dispose of the wastes, and at the same time, increases the level of magnetic frequency in the body as a more permanent process. In the body, the Q2 unit neutralizes both organic and inorganic toxins (heavy metals, chemical residues, and drugs). Some adverse skin blemishing has been reported when moisturizing cream was applied to the face of a woman, halfway through the treatment. This condition cleared upon cessation of cream application. Herbs, being an organic substance, may be considered exempt. Chemical medicines, antibiotics, and potions are considered to be toxins that the Q2 unit will attempt to neutralize, therefore delaying the healing process.

Method of Use

An individual doesn't need to be fully immersed in water to receive the full benefit of the Q2 system. A tub big enough for any limb could be used such as a copper tub which resonates on a physical and emotional level, or a quartz crystal bowl (hand) that resonates on a spiritual level (for advanced users). The most important thing about using this unit is that no matter what part of the body is in the water, the whole body will be affected. The Q2 unit is turned on for up to 35 minutes and generates negative electrons, which are released into the water as a waveform synergistic with the electrical state of the person being treated. The proprietary electronic circuitry ensures the energy waveform matches and enhances that of the individual in the water.

When some people start using this unit they experience a mild tingling or sensation at the site of old surgery or injuries. This is due to the area becoming energized. In some cases the condition may be of a long-term serious nature. Due to the increased energy levels the person may go into a temporary state whereby they become overstimulated. Also, any person experiencing a healing crisis may have some or all of the following symptoms: Muscle soreness; Tiredness (sleep for extraordinarily long period after treatment); Nausea or general unwell feeling or lethargy.

A healing crisis is when the body's natural defense systems are waging war on the illness itself, and the body is trying to purge the illness. During this time symptoms may worsen. However, this healing crisis will normally only last a few short days, and when it is over the body begins to heal very rapidly with improvements being extremely noticeable. The healing crisis is the most uncomfortable part of the process, but once it is over people have been simply astounded at how well they begin to feel.

Who should not use the Q2 system?

- People who have battery-operated implants (e.g., pace makers) should never use this unit. It has been documented that people

Who should not use the Q2 system?

- People who have battery-operated implants (e.g., pace makers) should never use this unit. It has been documented that people with such battery-operated implants should not be exposed to strong magnetic fields since these devices use magnetic impulses to operate. The Q2 unit creates its very own complex electromagnetic field. Therefore, using the Q2 unit could disable or damage the implant.
- Anyone who has received an organ transplant should not use the Q2. The reason being that those persons who have had an organ transplant are required to take antirejection drugs for survival. There is a possibility that the Q2 unit could extract these essential drugs from the body or it may enhance the person's immune system to such an extent that their body overrides the drugs. This same theory of drug extraction by the Q2 unit also applies to others that may be taking similar life-sustaining drugs.
- Pregnant women should not use the machine. The design of the unit allows it to work specifically on one bioentity (body) at a time. In the case of a pregnant woman, it is said that there are two completely separate bioentities, the mother and the fetus. Although these entities are contained in one body they still remain separate. Understanding why two people cannot share a bath can draw a clearer picture of why pregnant women cannot use the unit.

Recommended bathing time

Normal time in the bath is 25-35 minutes (maximum) based on one complete cycle of water (17 minutes). The body usually needs two cycles. The unit should be used **only** every second day for a period of one month. After that, the unit may be used once a week. People with certain compromised health conditions may need a reduced time on the unit at outset of therapy (25 to 35 minutes may be too long). The duration of bathing time is an individual determination based on what feels comfortable. Depending on condition, certain individuals may also need to use the Q2 every other day for a period of more than one month.

The electrode array causes basic electrolysis of the water, and gas bubbles are visible as they are released from the plates. The charging effect causes dissolved impurities in the water to be precipitated. This leads to discoloration of the water, sedimentation, and various odors (i.e., chlorine). What is interesting is that chlorine odor (which can change dramatically between different sessions) can be experienced using distilled water and no chloride-based salt. Perhaps what our senses are reading as chlorine could be reading some other gas. In some instances there are discernable odors that are experienced which upon questioning seem to correlate with something in the past of the person immersed in the session. These occurrences seem only to be explained as energetic exchanges and perhaps are not possible to chemically analyze.

It is very difficult to discern anything from the water's color change. It is a complex intermingling of the field of the person, the water, and the activated array (plates). If the water conditions are destabilizing to the plates, a cascade of electrolytic chemical reactions occur which result in the positive elements contributing mass, and the dissolved solids and chemicals in the water reacting. Add to this the field effects of the person, and complexity increases. As a person becomes more balanced and more coherent in their energy field, their energy field contributes less to the destabilization of the plates, resulting in less coloration in the water. As the body assimilates the bioenergy from the water, the body's innate intelligence will always direct its application. If detoxification is desired the process would be through the body's normal channels of elimination (urine, feces and perspiration.)

The usage of potassium citrate is very important. It helps increase the conductivity of the water, reduces the precipitation (brown-looking sludge) in the water and keeps the plates (in the orb) from wearing down.

Note: The innate intelligence of the body directs the deployment of the additional available bioenergy.

7
Electrolytes

Adequate hydration with a good mineral (electrolyte) supplement is beneficial, especially after using the Q2. When we are in good health, living organisms function in a state of exquisite balance. This equilibrium is known as homeostasis—the internal stability of electromagnetic and chemical systems within the body. Minerals are used to maintain homeostasis, but if these vital elements are missing, or delivered in a nonabsorbable form, homeostatic and bioelectric mechanisms break down potentially setting the stage for illness.

Many people are walking around in the grey zone of subclinical mineral deficiency. The true key to catalyzing the body's use of bioavailable minerals, speeding up remineralization, and restoring homeostasis is to use an ionic/crystalloid mineral solution, which works through a process of biovection. Crystalloid electrolytes are our body's energy source. Since we are vibrating beings, we must maintain an electrical charge that keeps our "batteries" running. The amplitude of our body's electricity alters in exact proportion to the amount of alkaline and acid-forming chemicals internally present at any one time. These electrochemicals influence the body's pH, which determines how effectively the biological systems run. When there is a deficiency of body electricity, our internal systems slow down and, in extreme cases of dehydration and mineral depletion eventually stop. Electrolytes are formed when specific minerals come together in solution and create electrical activity that provides energy for the body. When the electrolytes are dissolved in water they break apart into charged particles called ions. The ions carry either a negative or positive charge. It is these charged particles that create the electricity.

In my practice not only do I use the Q2 as part of the solution, I also recommend a specific trace mineral supplement. This formula is a "live" electrically charged mineral complex, which, because it is a crystalloid (a broken down ionic molecule), bypasses the digestive process and is immediately absorbed into the cell walls within minutes of being taken. Larger forms of minerals do not get the same results. In this form, the preventive and rejuvenative potential of trace minerals becomes infinite.

Comment from the author, Howard Peiper, N.D.

I have used crystalloid electrolytes (Trace-Lyte) in my clinical studies for many years treating patients suffering from long term, chronic disease and disabilities. When I started to incorporate using the Q2 Water Energy System with the electrolytes, the healing process was cut in half the time. I have noticed the following results: age spots fading, sinuses clearing, kidney function improved, general mental clarity, and headaches vanishing.

A subject suffering from gout and chronic back, joint, and leg pain for many years, with no relief from traditional or any other medicine received dramatic pain relief with all symptoms disappearing by the sixth footbath. My clients found a reduction in cold and flu symptoms and a faster recovery time using both the Q2 and the electrolytes

One of my clients had been suffering from extreme fluid retention in both of her ankles, knees, and hands for five years. By her third footbath treatment, along with taking oral electrolytes, a 90 percent reduction was observed. By the way, when I am using the Q2 unit on myself, I have noticed how my dog (Tashi) will either lie close to the footbath tub or will want to get into the bathtub with me. I really believe animals know and feel the electrical energy that is in the water. Even though I give her the electrolytes in her water, she still wants to be near the Q2 Water Energy System.

8
What People are Saying About the Q2

Because of the Q2 Water Energy System's ability to improve a body's biocharge, practitioners and their patients who use the device have reported numerous benefits. Some of the aspects that have been reported include:
- increased vitality
- revitalized blood
- detoxification and neutralization of toxins
- pain and stress relief
- faster recovery time from illness or injury
- reduced inflammation
- improved sleep
- reduced fluid retention
- improved endocrine and metabolic function
- elimination of menstrual pain
- dermal rejuvenation
- improved kidney and liver function

The following reports are clinical observations that have been reported by health care practitioners from all over the world.

"We have been using the Q2 Water Energy System in our clinic for more than 3 months as an integral part of our overall treatment. Many of our clients come to us with symptoms caused by food intolerances and vitamin and mineral deficiencies, which are frequently treated by exclusion diets and supplementation. We find the Q2 to be extremely effective in giving the resultant detoxification process a vigorous kickstart, which speeds the client on the road to recovery. Pre-post Q2 treatment tests have shown toxin level reduction of more than 25 percent after only a half hour's treatment with the Q2.

We also use the Q2 Water Energy System as an adjunct to Lymphatic drainage massage, which often leaves the patient tired, listless, and in a state of low energy. The Q2 is particularly effective in revitalizing such patients. Many patients also find the Q2 helpful for the same reasons. The beauty of the Q2 is in its ease of operation and the fact that once the treatment commences it requires no intervention from the operator, who can continue with other duties or treatments at the same time."
- *Biotech Health & Nutrition Centre, U.K.*

"I have introduced the Q2 Water Energy System to some of my clients over the past few weeks. As a Kinesiologist, I assess and strengthen energy unbalances, work with the physical, emotional, intuitional, and energy aspects of the whole being. I have used Kinesiology testing to check clients before and after taking a Q2 footbath. These tests show a consistent increase in available energy for healing, balanced meridian energy, and balanced chakras after the bath. I am very pleased with the results."
- *Parijat Wismer, Kinesiologist, and Herbalist, U.K.*

"As a Natural Health Practitioner, I have been using the Q2 Water Energy System for more than 2 years now, and can honestly say that I have never encountered a more powerful healing tool. Initially skeptical, it took only a few baths to dispel my doubts completely. As a Specialized Kinesiologist, I am able to use muscle testing to establish exactly what the bath has done, the results were so outstanding I actually questioned my testing until I got used to the "miracles" the unit produces.

I have spent the last two years extensively documenting the progress results of the unit on my clients. These results never cease to amaze and impress me. The unit has become such an integral part of my healing work that I can't imagine being without it. Where possible I always put my clients in the bath first to allow it to do the bulk of the balancing. Then I follow the bath with a healing session. The combination of bath and session is life changing to the point where I literally guarantee results.

I heartily recommend the Q2 Water Energy System to all Natural Health Practitioners, as long as they have a method of testing the client to ensure no possible detriment will ensue (as with any healing tool there is always a minority, particularly those taking prescription drugs, who may have an adverse reaction to the treatment). In my opinion, the Q2 unit is, without question or qualification, the best investment you will ever make."
- *Samantha-Joy McCormick, N.D., Austin, TX*

"My name is Pedro V. DeCosta and I have been a K-12 teacher in Calif. since 1976. My work has been mostly at the primary level, and I have also worked with special education children, namely the autistic. I have worked with children with mild to severe perceptual-motor disabilities, using alternative physical therapy. The following report is my personal testimony regarding the astonishing progress that I have witnessed take place in the life of an austistic seven-year-old boy, ever since using the Q2 Water Energy System. His parents started giving him a Q2 bath every other day as of January 29, 2000. The results were instant. The first bath was given just before he received his daily session of occupational therapy at his house (it used to be three hours in duration and is now only two hours and going down).

He was unusually calm and to the therapist's surprise, did every task with 100 percent accuracy. He was cooperative, cheerful in contrast to his normal erratic, noncompliant, restless behavior. From that first day on, he kept progressing with major achievements, which I documented. Currently he is nearly eight-years old and will be entering third grade. He looks and acts like any other normal eight-year-old, except for some speech impediments, which are being corrected through his therapy and class work. Everyone who sees him, including the parents of other autistic children, cannot believe this is the same child from a few months ago.

Personally having known this young boy prior to January—a restless, stressed out, uncooperative child—I stand in awe of the child he has become—pleasant, bright, talkative, good humored, cooperative, and alert. That is my humble prognosis as a teacher of 25 years working with thousands of children in various school

districts in California. My personal belief is that the Q2 Water Energy System baths have allowed this lad to calm down and concentrate on his tasks, allowing him to learn properly what he is taught. This has also led to a compounding effect, accelerating his progress in all academic areas as well as those of general physical, emotional, and social development."
- *Pedro V. DeCosta, Teacher, Whittier, CA*

"I am a Health Kinesiology (HK) practitioner. HK is an original and comprehensive system of body/mind/spirit energy work and has a broad application range from electromagnetic issues to psychological and spiritual ones, and from allergy to detoxification. The way I work is according to what we call body priority. The body's own innate intelligence knows what its most urgent and appropriate concerns are. I address these with HK, layer by layer, so to speak.

I have been seeing some very interesting, and I would actually call them amazing, results in the indexing numbers I do for my clients who have taken advantage of the Q2 Water Energy System before their HK sessions. The use of the Q2 unit increases the basic available healing energy in the body. Here I share three of my recent Q2 and HK sessions:

One client's energy state of health for her lymphatic system was 4 percent before using the Q2 and 91 percent after using it. Then HK work brought it up to 99 percent. The energy state of her muscular system was 31 percent and the Q2 brought it up to 94 percent. Another client's body needed to address the energy state of her glandular system. The numbers were 32 percent before Q2 and 81 percent after, then HK brought it up to 98 percent.

Yet another client had a particularly stressful weekend and when she came in for her appointment the energy state of health for her nervous system was only 1 percent, the Q2 brought it up to 35 percent, and then HK work brought it up to 96 percent.

Using the Q2 Water Energy System has opened up more possibilities for my work since my clients who use it have increased energy potential to work with."
- *Jackie Plugge, H.K, Columbus, NE*

"The following are testimonies of some of the clients I have helped with the Q2 Water Energy System and Nutritional Supplements:

A thirty-six-year-old male had extreme adrenal exhaustion; his kidneys, thyroid, and thymus were failing. By the third bath, his body was responding with more energy. After bath #18 his mental fog was gone. Occasionally he gets tired and still takes Thymus for stress. His daughter (nineteen) had two foot baths and all the warts fell off her hands, her mental capabilities improved, and her kidney pain was gone as long as she takes the bath two times a week along with the glandular supplement identified as *Kidney*.

A forty-three-year-old female had very bad seasonal allergies. Head congestion, nausea, and fatigue got her down every spring. She started the footbaths three weeks before the season hit. She lives on a farm with animals and every weed you can imagine. She experienced absolutely no allergy reaction at all! She was able to go out with the horses, something she had not done in years. She brought her daughter in for a footbath. Her daughter had a bone cyst approximately four inches long in her calf. It was noticeable and had been there for a long time. After the first bath we all just stared at her leg—the cyst had gone down by about 50 percent.

Another fifty-six-year-old female had 21 baths, in addition to her nutritional program, and exhibited the following results. She had tender breasts and a lump in the right breast. All lumps were gone in six baths. Insomnia resolved in three baths, dandruff in nine baths. Her eyes were so sensitive to light and after three baths this was no longer an issue. She recently brought her husband in. His right foot was solid blue with varicose veins. He has had twelve baths and his varicose foot is the same color as his left foot. You can still see the blue veins but it is hardly noticeable.

I have two dogs who love to be in the Q2 bath. One who used to snore and after just the first bath does not snore anymore. The other dog has skin allergies and was hyper. After putting her in the bath for the first time, she calmed down and eventually curled up on the carpet and slept. Her allergies are much better."

- *Teresa Henderson, C.H., N.D., Salem, OR*

"The Q2 Water Energy System has consistently given me the feeling of overall well-being and lightness. I have more energy and my ability to concentrate has greatly improved. My clients have all reported positive results from regular use of the Q2, including quick improvement from long standing bacterial infection, more balanced energy levels, and improved emotional outlooks."
- *Tara Ishaya, QXCI Practitioner and Herbalist,*
Virginia Beach, VA

"As a natural health practitioner, I have to try everything on myself (and my family) first. I bought a Q2 unit for my husband and myself. Both of us do a fair amount of traveling in airplanes which bombards you with radiation, plus the hazard of changes in water, restaurant food with high bacterial count and food poisoning residue, and just plenty of foreign materials that you do not find in your home. It takes a lot more work to stay balanced and keep the immune system strong while traveling, so I was interested in the Q2 for regeneration of cellular energy. We can *really* feel the difference. We feel stronger and are staying up later and getting up earlier. The first client who had the Q-Experience had a thirty-year history of foot problems. He said he felt like dancing after his first treatment! This is quite a tool for our time."
- *Rose Mary Camren, N.D., Woodinville, WA*

"The following are several reports using the Q2 Water Energy System on my patients:

The first lady, aged twenty-seven, had a breast removed seven years earlier and was in very poor condition. With the "staph" being resistant to antibiotics, she was left with a yellow open wound on the area. It took six baths to clear up the condition. In her case, she had a moderately severe healing crisis that prolonged the time delay between the first few baths. She is now back to good health.

As the Q2 Water Energy System unit works on a cellular DNA level, the benefits are confined to organic and synthetic toxins with all their known pathological side effects. The realigning of the meridians to give a hormonal balance eliminates all the symptoms known under the term premenstrual tension.

Several women who have suffered all their life, some with up to five days of cramps, migraines, and mood swings, were relieved of these symptoms after their first bath on day one of the cycle. The next menstrual cycle was also treated with the same results. By the third cycle, with one young woman who had particularly bad five-day menses, no extra treatment was necessary. The PMT was replaced by an increased feeling of wellbeing and vitality."
- *Georgia Martin, N.D., Concord, NH*

"Procedures and Methods:
Each patient was to take a 20-35 minute bath, depending on how they felt physically and emotionally within themselves while in the bath. Regular temperature city water was used and the Q2 unit was placed in the bath with the patient.

Report Summary:
Trials were conducted in an ordinary household bathtub. Bathtub was thoroughly cleaned after each treatment.
➤ Case 1: Patient felt relief of pain and increase of mobility in joints. The lack of mobility was due mostly to severe arthritis in the hands. Case one had a total of three baths and reported improvements immediately after each treatment.
➤ Case 2: Felt no specific improvement straight after the bath but reported a much higher energy level the next day.
➤ Case 3: Patient had suffered chronic pain for at least twelve years, related to arthritis, bad kidneys, possible lupus, high blood pressure, artificial hip, and bad back. Subject had taken a homeopathic remedy, *Panadine Forte* for at least a year to lessen the pain. Large improvements were reported in reducing the pain immediately after each bath and the patient noticed large increases of energy. Subject also had a rather severe rash covering the right side of the abdomen and both hands before starting treatment. Patient's sleeping patterns improved by the third bath and also had reported softer skin, and a decrease in menopause flashes. Subject quite often experienced some pain or tingling sensations during baths that would dissipate after exiting the bath. By the end of fifteen treatments patient had experienced a decrease in blood pressure and rash had

completely vanished. Subject reported feeling free of pain and quite wonderful. Subject had ceased taking her homeopathic remedy as she commented there was no need for them.
- Case 5: Subject suffered fluid retention in hands, legs, and feet, also a pain in hands and lack of energy. Reported feeling some pain, tingling, and tightening feelings during baths that vanished after exiting the bath. A large reduction of pain was reported after each bath. By the sixth bath, patient reported increased mobility plus 90 percent reduction in prominent scars.
- Case 6: Patient quite often reported pain and tingling sensations during bath that would vanish upon exiting the bath. She suffered from severe menstrual cramps and low blood pressure. Subject reported complete relief of all menstrual cramps by the ninth bath, had also noticed dramatic fading of scar tissue, and had noticed a rise in blood pressure.
- Case 7: Patient suffered from incontinence and aches and pains. Often reported pain or tingling during baths that disappeared upon exiting the bath. Subject reported relief of pain felt immediately after each treatment and an increase in energy felt the next day.
- Case 8: Subject was suffering from a hernia—reported reduction in pain immediately after bath. Next day subject noted hernia was softer and reduction in swelling.
- Case 9: Patient suffered from Chronic Fatigue Syndrome. Subject experienced extreme dizziness during first bath. The dizziness persisted through each treatment and disappeared after baths. It was recommended that the subject hop out of the bath when the dizziness started. By bath nine, the subject was able to stay in bath for twenty minutes before the dizziness occurred. After each bath subject reported relief of aches and pains.

Overall Observations

During the course of these trials it was observed that pains, tingling sensations, etc. were mainly experienced in areas of the body that centered the cause of the illness or injuries. These sensations always dissipated after baths and resulted in relief of original problem (i.e., pain). It was also observed that each individual's bath water proved to be a different color and texture after treatment.

Color of individual's bath water also changed over the course of baths. During these trials it was noted that high blood pressure read lower after Q2 treatments and low blood pressure often read higher after treatments. Best results were achieved when follow up baths were taken. All subjects reported some benefits no matter how many or few baths they took."
- *Center for Integrated Healing, Los Angeles, CA*

"Each Q2 session is like standing in the ocean and drinking in all of the energy flowing around me. For twenty-five years, I have taken natural health products and had fairly good results, however, I was never satisfied and felt something was missing. After six sessions with the Q2 Water Energy System, I realized what was missing; the spark that ignites everything I do for my body, mind, and spirit. With each session my energy increases, I feel more at peace, and I am more excited about living life to the fullest. I can feel my body relax as I release toxins, and my mind race with new ideas as I release my negative thinking. I have not felt this good in decades."
- *Ann Benoit, Nutrition Consultant and Crystal Healer, Peachtree City, GA*

"It's hard to believe how good I feel now when I get up in the morning. I'm not stiff and sore. I had polio as a baby and have always walked with crutches. But since I began using the Q2 Water Energy System, the most amazing things have been happening. I have been forgetting to use my crutches!!! I am actually feeling tingling in my wasted muscles after all these years."
- *Ed Dalpe, Quantum & Massage Therapist, Redford, MI*

"I have been using the Q2 Water Energy System every other day for the last month and the benefits have been enormous. I'm feeling a much greater sense of wellbeing and balance all day and well into the evening. I feel a great deal more joy—the joy of being alive. I'm feeling my senses more activated and heightened. I also feel much more open and loving and as a result I am drawing more love and support into my life. And I'm noticing that my ability to visualize and manifest what I want in my life is more effective and

faster. I am finding myself to be infinitely more creative and intuitive and have a great new knowing that all is well in my life. What could be better?"
- *Ingrid Mueller, Nurse in Private Alternative Medicine Practice, Macomb, MI*

"After an auto accident and brain concussion a year ago, my world looked very drab. My ability to think and even speak had been seriously altered. The first time I stepped into the quantum field, I felt as if my life were being given back to me. People who know me say my "sparkle" has returned, because the Q2 Water Energy System and an ancient formula that I take. My health, happiness, clarity, and joy are back. And I have gained a deeper connection to an awareness of nature and the wonder of all living things."
- *Karen Justice, Author, Networker, and Designer, New York, NY*

"I thought I would let you know that I have received great benefit from using the Q2 Water Energy System. In particular, the lessening of Chronic Fatigue Syndrome symptoms, elimination of stiffness, soreness, and pain from Fibromyalgia, no more foot and leg cramps, and significant detoxifying. (I had been exposed to chemicals, heavy metals.)
Author's Note: One does need to support the liver and bowels during this process.
      Over the years I have spent thousands of dollars and swallowed thousands of supplements, the majority with little noticeable effect. That is what I like about your device—it works. The benefits are significant, noticeable, and increase with regular use of the unit. By the way, it appears that my hormonal system is slowly being reactivated at age 52."
- *Carol Clarke, Lansing, MI*

"Thank you so much for introducing me to the Q2 Water Energy System and Trace-Lyte (electrolytes). I have been dealing with stress and trying to balance my life for many years. After my first bath with the Q2, I found myself feeling very blissful and at peace.

I feel I'm staying a lot more peaceful and relaxed. My "batteries" are staying charged and my energy is great."
- *Meg Cassell, Musician and Teacher, Albuquerque, NM*

"After having been on the Q2 Water Energy System 3 times I have to say WOW! It made me feel so much better, and it even enhanced my psychic abilities. I have decided the Q2 is something I really don't want to live without."
- *Rev. Jack Butler, World Renown Psychic Counselor and Minister, Tampa, FL*

"The intention of this letter is to give testimony of the wonderful results obtained by using the unit called Q2 Water Energy System. This incredible machine has given amazing results to my brother (age 40) in dealing with his health problems. Three years ago my brother was diagnosed with a very aggressive form of prostate cancer. His cancer is in remission now, but due to high dosages of chemotherapy, he consequently lost his kidneys. He receives dialysis every other day. After every session he is extremely tired and frequently has a high temperature. Two years ago, his doctor suggested a blood transfusion to alleviate the risk of developing leukemia.

Two months ago, my brother started to use the Q2 unit and these are the results obtained: His blood level went up from 27.4 to 40.1 (forty being the highest level possible in this category). His energy level is so high that he is able to resume daily activities right after the dialysis session and he is no longer forced to take medication to bring the fever down. Another condition that improved noticeably was that my brothers left foot completely recovered. Due to the location and nature of the cancer, part of his lower spinal cord was affected and the mobility and sensation of the toes was lost. Although the doctor stated this condition was irreversible, he doesn't need his walking cane anymore. We are very grateful to God, our Creator, for having the Q2 Water Energy System and its makers come into our lives."
- *Alicia Binares, Dallas, TX*

"I have been using the Q2 Water Energy System unit for six weeks and I have noticed several changes in my body, such as improved sleeping patterns, subtle and toned skin, and greatly increased well-being and energy. I have also noticed a dramatic improvement in my cardiovascular system. For instance I was beginning to develop a smokers cough and this has now completely vanished. I have also found that I can run up stairs without being out of breath. I had been suffering from severe skin cancer, the smallest of which has disappeared and the larger one greatly reduced in size. I highly recommend the Q2 unit for general good health and wellbeing and also for chronic illnesses."
- *Steve Allen, Toowoomba, Queesnland, AU*

"My personal experience with the Q2 unit convinces me that I would not want to be without it. Medical people are trying to diagnose me with Crohn's Disease and the Q2 keeps me going. I am dealing with the diet and allergy issues, rest, exercise, etc. and the Q2 does something I can't explain. All the biopsies indicate that there is an absence of the usual tissue changes that usually accompany Crohn's. Other people who have used the Q2 have reported various results. One man had severe, crippling arthritis pain, and got out of the Q2 bath with a 95 percent reduction in pain. Another man who had a high PSA test (3.6), after using the Q2 three times his next test result was 1.8."
- *Althea Dixon, Glendale, AZ*

"Approximately six months ago a blood test revealed that my husband's iron count was well above the norm. (Too much iron in the tissues and organs leads to free radicals and increases the need for vitamin E. High levels of iron have been found in association with heart disease and cancer). His doctor recommended that he give a pint of blood on three separate occasions to help alleviate the problem. My husband only went once, meanwhile I received my Q2 unit and began using it on him. I am happy to report that his doctor was left scratching his head in wonderment when he received my husband's latest lab results. His iron count was totally normal and the doctor wasn't able to give a reason for it. He should

have asked me because I knew the Q2 unit was responsible for this most positive change."
- *Madeline Bresner, Bellevue, WA*

"I used my Q2 Water Energy System on Monday, had an eyelid-lift on Wednesday, used the Q2 that day and again on Friday. When I had the stitches removed on the following Monday, the surgeon was very impressed at the amount of healing that had taken place in such a short period of time. I also noticed that my skin felt much tighter and smoother. I also had a cyst on my leg that I'd had for forty-five years, and on that day I noticed it had disappeared. Being sixty-five, I had some brown spots on my hands and they are slowly fading. People ask me how I can look younger each time they see me. I feel energized each time I use the Q2. I thank God and you every day for this wonderful discovery. It will be a part of my life from now on."
- *Lily Rambo, Bigfork, MT*

"With reference to the Q2 Water Energy System and what it means to my wife and I, may I say that we are more than satisfied with the results we have noticed in relation to our problems of sun cancer since using the Q2 unit. First, my wife had a large sun cancer on her left forearm, which she has been treating for several years now with very little visual results of cure with the many lotions, potions, etc. that she has used. After only a few weeks of bathing with the Q2 unit, she has been amazed to see the sun cancer in question shrivel and totally disappear.

I, too, have had a sun cancer on the right side of my head near the temple. This has been a source of annoyance for me for a number of years in that I had to be careful when combing my hair and when going out in the sun, especially when swimming. I also noticed that after just a few baths using the Q2, the cancer started to shrink and eventually fell off. At the same time a new and previously unseen sun cancer appeared on my left forearm, which very quickly came to the surface, dried up, and also fell off.

We have noticed that our skin is looking much clearer since beginning the Q2 treatment and we would thoroughly recommend its use for a better, clearer and cleaner, skin. Sun cancers are no

longer a concern for us, as we now know what to do and how to rid ourselves of this problem."
- *Don & Cherrie McCollom*, *Birkdale, Queensland, AU*

"I am an energy worker. I got the Q2 Water Energy System to explore its benefits, after finding the way it works is aligned with how I work, thus shaking out energetics that accumulate not only in the physical body but in the subtle bodies as well. I find it depletes mineral content in my body and I am using a electrolyte (crystalloid) supplement to rebalance my body. In my opinion, the Q2 is of great service as it "moves energy" easily, on a daily basis as a part of life. This includes emotional congestion!"
- *Chely's Natural Therapeutics*, *Albuquerque, NM*

"I am sure the Q2 Water Energy System has helped to detox my body. Sometimes when I was doing it every other day in the bathtub, I got negative sensations (headaches). Therefore, I changed to using the footbath while continuing my regimen of fourteen baths per twenty-eight days. I also saw in a live blood analysis how it pulled the acid out of my blood bringing it to a proper pH. It also pulled lots of impurities out of my blood with a noticeable difference between visual before and after blood samples. I am currently taking a crystalloid electrolyte to help maintain my pH balance. What a combination, the Q2 unit and Trace-Lyte."
- *Florence Jeff*, *Orlando, FL*

"A 1998 motor vehicle accident resulted in large blood clots in my leg, which produced leg ulcers and skin discoloration. After six treatments the Q2 unit definitely made a noticeable difference in leg ulcers and skin discoloration."
- *Rick Laurenzi*, *Denver, CO*

"I am fifty-six and have suffered from arthritis and terrible leg cramps for about ten years now. These began when I contracted the Ross River Virus in 1990. I gave up my nursing career because of the arthritis and the inability to walk for any length of time. The leg cramps were so bad some nights I had hardly any sleep. Since I worked full-time in an office job, I would get very tired during the

day. I did not believe the Q2 Water Energy System would work, but after a few baths I found moving easier and can honestly say my life has changed. I very seldom get leg cramps, my arthritis, although still present, is no longer a major issue and I find walking a lot easier. I have tried all sorts of cures. I was a very active person and I am once more doing things I haven't done in years. My quality of life has improved. Although I still find it hard to believe, I thought I was destined to a life of pain and confinement. It *really* does work."
- **Lexie Cook**, Toronto, ON

"In 1994 I was diagnosed with multiple myeloma. I was in denial and being a member of the elite forces of our military, I was in almost perfect physical and mental condition. When I retired in 1999 I was treated for pneumonia. The treatment did not seem to improve my condition and I returned to the Veterans Hospital to receive a more effective treatment. The lab results showed my white blood cells were almost gone and my red blood cells were cut in half. In other words, my bone marrow was 95 percent filled with cancer—non-Hodgkin's lymphoma, Grade IV lymphoplasmacytic lymphoma. I was admitted to the hospital and for twenty-five days where I received daily transfusions of whole blood. I was not expected to live very long. When I was discharged from the hospital, my very good friend Michael Stern loaned me a Q machine. After each treatment with the Q machine I sensed that something positive was happening to me. I could feel energy returning in a very positive way. When I received electrodermal screening I could see my energy returning to a balanced position due to the Q machine. After six months of Q treatments my cancer went into remission and has been in remission since December 2000.

It is my sincere belief that while I continue to use the Q machine I will remain in a balanced condition, my immune system will work efficiently, and the cancer will never return."
-**Daniel Costigan**, Lt.Col. Ret., *Bloomington, MN*

A: Research Report

"Q - The Experience" Scientifically Evaluated Mood and Brain Wave Testing Before and After Q-Footbaths.

Dr. James V. Hardt
Biocybernaut Institute, Inc.
San Francisco, Ca.
October 16, 2002

Introduction: The purpose of this study was to begin to discover and to understand the range of effects of the Q-The Experience ("Q") technology when it is used with human subjects and to examine the Q effects on alpha brain waves (EEG) and on moods and emotions.

Design: The study design was a single blind crossover design with thirty subjects randomly assigned to have either a Placebo footbath or a Q footbath for 35 minutes on each of two days, with one day in between the two sessions. If a given subject was in the *Placebo* group on the first session, this same subject was in the *Treatment* group on the second session and vice versa. Batteries of personality tests were given on the first day. On both days, blood pressure was measured and subjective pain reports were collected 6 times per day. Computerized mood scale assessments were made three times per day to assess moods before, during, and after the footbath.
    Following each day's first mood scale (which was recorded as the before mood scale), there were three EEG baselines in which EEG activity was recorded from eight cortical locations. The EEG activity at each cortical location was filtered into eight different filter bands, including Broad Band Alpha, which was the EEG data used in the analysis for this study. At each of the eight cortical locations the eight filter bands (64 total channels of data) were scored by computer to assess the integrated amplitude scores which were quantified every fifteen seconds. The Pre-footbath EEG baseline conditions were Eyes Open (EO) (with lights on), Eye Closed (EC) (in the dark) and White Noise (WN) (also in the

dark). Following these three Pre-footbath EEG baselines (EO, EC, WN), subjects were given a 35-minute footbath using tap water that had been heated to between 105 and 108 degrees Fahrenheit immediately after the footbath. With their feet still in the water, subjects completed the "during" mood scale to describe how they felt during the footbath. Then the three EEG baselines were repeated to have post-footbath EEG measures. The subjects then completed the final "after" mood scale to describe how they felt right at that moment, now that the experience was over.

Procedure: The Placebo condition was identical procedurally to the Q Treatment condition except that the running (i.e. plugged in and turned on) power supply was not connected to the "Energizer Unit." This unit contains the ring disk plates that is always inserted into the water between the subject's feet. Members of the placebo group were unaware that only one of their two days was a Q Treatment footbath and the other day was a "dummy." Only the laboratory director knew which subjects were receiving which condition on any given day.

Method (Equipment): All peripheral modality data (heart rate, blood pressure) were collected with an Omron automatic inflation electronic digital pressure/pulse monitoring system. All EEG data were collected with either a Biocybernaut Institute Mark 8 Hybrid Spectral Analysis system or a Biocybernaut Institute Mark 9 DSP-based Digital Spectral Analysis, both with 64 channels of A/D converted signals. The Biocybernaut Institute computerized mood scales were given three times each day. The first administration ("Pre") was before the footbath with instructions to describe how the person felt "right now." This was followed by three EEG baselines (EO, EC, WN) and then the footbath was given for 35 minutes. Immediately after the footbath, and while their feet were still in the warm water, subjects completed the second set of computerized mood scales (during), with instructions to describe how they felt during the footbath. Then the three EEG baselines were run again. This was followed by the third and final computerized mood scale (post), which asked subjects to describe how they felt "right now."

Results: It would appear the Q treatment has powerful anxiety-reducing effects that begin to appear within 20 minutes following the Q-Treatment footbath, at which time the final "after" mood scale was administered. When anxiety-reducing effects are exhibited, initially they are unconscious. In order to understand how the effects of the Q-Treatment footbath develop over time we must note the increase of two different measures of depression in the treatment group, relative to the placebo group. Recall that the time of the post-footbath mood scale is about 20 minutes after the end of the footbath. Anxiety has shown to significantly decrease in the treatment group, relative to the placebo control group. Anyone who has worked with the Q-Experience technology has seen a melancholy mood develop in the subjects during the minutes and hours after their first experience, and is considered a quantified scientific description of the after effects.

Even more intriguing is the fact that the subjects can simultaneously feel less energy and at the same time can feel stronger and more robust as defined in the post-treatment group relative to the post-placebo group. The difference may be potential wellbeing vs. energy to actualize that potential which are the effects seen at the 20-minute point following the footbath. There is a very strong set of indicators that the Q Experience process produces strong and beneficial changes in mood and emotions two days following just one 35-minute treatment. If broadly applied across the population, these types of results could well lead to beneficial changes in the way people feel and perhaps in the ways they relate to each other. The reductions in anxiety, depression and unhappiness are also powerful and potentially beneficial to almost every area of human behavior. These very strong statistical results reveal the powerful and beneficial effects of just one 35-minute Q-Treatment on moods and emotions.

Summary: The Q-Treatment significantly increases Eyes-Closed EEG Alpha activity at selected cortical sites, especially occipital sites, and the also reduces negative emotions including anxiety, depression, unhappiness and hostility. These favorable changes to subject moods become stronger over the following two days as indicated by this study. The studies also show beneficial short-term effects of the Q-Treatment, such as increases of amiable emotions, clear thinking, and strong and robust energy. It may well be that additional treatments beyond the one Q-Treatment would lead to longer-term increases of the positive moods created. Careful attention has been given to identifying the subjects in this research study so they could be solicited for more extensive studies. Firmly established by the results of this study are the longer-term (2 days post-treatment) reductions in negative moods including anxiety, depression, unhappiness and hostility being immediately apparent. Further studies could assess whether there are also long-term improvements in the positive emotions that would develop with subsequent Q-Treatments.

♈

In closing it must be said many people are achieving wondrous results using the Q2 Water Energy System unit. There are many devices out in the market place claiming miraculous things, but the Q2 unit is different from all of them because it was designed with its specific purpose already determined. It was never an accidental discovery and is based solidly on medical facts. The device utilizes the technology of "Q," which is rapidly becoming the new science of the world.

RESOURCE DIRECTORY

Q2 Water Energy System
Q-Tech Laboratories from Australia has developed the most advanced hydrotherapy treatment on the planet. Founded by Terry Skrinjar, an amazing inventor who started designing highly advanced technology when he was five years old. Q-Tech has created the process that unleashes the capacity for water to transform electric energy into Life Force Energy. By being in contact with the water during the process, your body is able to assimilate this Bio energy and then utilize the energy as it sees fit. Once your body has the energy it needs to work with, its restoration/regeneration capacity is recovered. The results are astonishing. If you have seen either the movie *Cocoon* or *Tuck Everlasting* then you have an idea of the concept.
    Trace-Lyte. This supplement is a true crystalloid (smallest form in nature) electrolyte formula that helps maintain the body's primary bio-oxidation process. It raises the Osmotic Pressure of the cell walls, strengthening them! It also changes back the pH of the cell to its healthy state. High absorption is achieved due to its crystalloid structure. Unlike most earth-type liquid minerals, there are no heavy metal contaminants whatsoever.
    ElectroBlast.™ The same Trace-Lyte electrolyte formula in an easy-to-carry effervescent tablet. When dissolved in cold or hot water makes a great-tasting lemon-lime drink, without sugar or artificial sweeteners. Includes stevia and vitamin C.
    Copper Tubs. Available from The Q The Experience

"Advanced Products for an Advancing World"
Q-The Experience

(888)-309-5703 www.Q2.com.au

Quartz Crystal Hand Bowls
Available through Environmental Technology (800)-827-0762
www.futurewatertoday.com

Index

A-K

Australia, 21, 51
bathing time, 31
bioelectrical field, 29
bioenergy, 32
bio-magnetic healing, 17
cell membrane, 19, 20, 21, 24
Chinese Medicine, 11, 13
crystalloid, 33, 48, 49, 51
detoxification, 32, 35, 38
diet, 2
Dis-ease, 12, 13
Einstein, 11
electrolytes, 33, 45, 49, 50
energy, 3, 4, 9, 10, 11, 12, 13, 16, 17, 19, 20, 21, 23, 24, 27, 28, 29, 30, 32, 33, 35, 36, 38, 39, 40, 41, 42, 43, 45, 46, 48, 50, 51
healing crisis, 30, 40
healing waters, 9, 10
homeostasis, 33, 51
immune system, 24, 29, 31, 40
innate intelligence, 32, 38
intercellular fluid, 19, 20, 21
kidneys, 16, 19, 21, 29, 39, 41, 45
Kinesiology, 36, 38

L-Z

life force, 23
Live Blood Test, 24
liver, 15, 16, 19, 21, 29, 35, 44
Lourdes, 9
magnetic field, 27, 31
Medjugorje, 9
minerals, 17, 23, 33, 51
negative electrons, 30
Newtonian, 11
organ transplant, 31
plasma membrane, 19, 21
Q2, 4, 7, 10, 20, 21, 24, 25, 27, 28, 29, 30, 31, 33, 35, 36, 37, 38, 39, 40, 41, 43, 44, 45, 46, 47, 48, 49, 50, 51
Q2 Water Energy System, 7, 10, 20, 21, 24, 25, 27, 28, 35, 36, 37, 38, 39, 40, 43, 44, 45, 46, 47, 48, 49, 50, 51
sine wave, 28
Ste. Anne de Beaupres, 9
toxins, 10, 16, 17, 19, 20, 21, 29, 35, 41, 43

Bibliography

-Beck, Robert, *The Body Electric*, Putnam Pub., 1986.
-Gerber, Richard, *Practical Guide to Vibrational Medicine*, Harper Collins, 2000.
-Marsh, Richard, "Report on the New BEFE Unit," Explore Magazine, Vol. 10, #6, 2001.
-Martlew, Gillian, *Electrolytes, The Spark of Life*, Nature's Publishing, 1998.
-Mirman, R., "Quantum Field Theory," Nova Science, 2001.
-Nature's Journal #392, p. 734-737, 1998.
-Ray, Timothy, OMD, L.Ac, *The Low Battery Focus*, Explore, Vol 10, #4, 2001.
-Reid, Daniel, *The Tao of Detox,* Chapter 9: High-Tech Electro-Detox, Cygnus Books 2003.
-Skrinjar, T., Walker, S, *Q Mechanics*, Skrinjar-Walker Publishing, 1996.
-Smith, Lendon, *Feed Your Kids Right*, Keats Publishing, 1986.

Other Books available through ATN Publishing

Nutritional Leverage for Great Golf $ 9.95
Improving your score on the back nine.

Eliminating Pilot Error $ 7.95
The final step in flight training.

The Backseat Flyer $ 9.95
What every passenger should know about flying.

2012 Airborne Prophesy $16.95
A suspense novel about the future and electromagnetic mind weapons.

Spirit and Creator (hardcover) $39.95
The Man behind Lindbergh's Flight to Paris.

Analyzing Sports Drinks $ 4.95
Carbohydrates or Electrolytes. Which is right for you?

Kiss Your Life Hello $ 9.95
Health and Recovery with PSP

*For a complete listing of books by ATN Publishing
and Safe Goods Publishing visit our web site:
safegoodspub.com
or call for a free catalog (888) 628-8731
order line: (888) NATURE-1*